Caring KITTEN

by Andrea McHugh

The DALMATIAN PRESS name and logo are
trademarks of Dalmatian Press, LLC, Franklin, Tennessee 37067.
No part of this book may be reproduced or copied in any form
without the written permission of Dalmatian Press, LLC.
Cover Photo by Sharon Eide and Elizabeth Flynn /sandephoto.com
Interior Photos © Amanda Bulbeck
Editor *Mary Ginder*
Designer *Dan Waters*
ISBN: 1-40370-886-X

13470 Caring For Your Kitten
04 05 06 07 08 WWP 10 9 8 7 6 5 4 3 2 1

About the Author

Andrea McHugh is a cat lover whose life has been enriched over the years by cats and kittens of all shapes and sizes, each of whom has had its own unique personality. She combined her love of writing with her love of cats as sub-editor on the best-selling *Your Cat* magazine and regularly attended veterinary and animal behavior conferences, becoming fascinated by all aspects of feline care.

Today she works as a freelance journalist, specializing in writing for pet publications.

McHugh lives in Lincolnshire, England, with her daughter, Madeline, and her partner, Mark, a veterinarian. She also shares her home with a handsome red Persian called Rufus.

Contents

CHOOSING A KITTEN

Congratulations! By reading this book you are taking the first step to learn about the care and training of your kitten, which means you are well on the way to becoming a responsible cat owner. Few things in the world are as beautiful or entertaining as a new kitten; but, by inviting one of these enchanting creatures to share your life, you are making a big commitment. Sadly, animal shelters are full of cats whose owners did not fulfill their responsibilities.

When you accept a kitten into your home, you are responsible for his well-being for the rest of his life.

Responsibilities of Ownership

To be a responsible cat owner you need to:

- Understand your kitten's needs and consider whether your lifestyle and budget can accommodate them.
- Arrange veterinary care and ensure your kitten is vaccinated against disease and wormed regularly.
- Prevent unwanted litters by getting your kitten neutered when he or she is old enough.
- Provide your kitten with a well-balanced diet, opportunities for exercise, and regular grooming.
- Provide the kitten with identification such as microchipping.
- Make arrangements for your kitten to be cared for whenever you will be away from home.

WHY ARE THERE SO MANY CATS IN SHELTERS?
Lost or abandoned cats are the consequence of impulse buying, failure to spay or neuter (which results in unwanted kittens), and lack of proper identification to make it possible to reunite stray cats with their owners.

What Kind of Kitten Is Right for Your Lifestyle?

Bringing a kitten home should not be an impulsive decision. To make sure that everyone in the home will be pleased, including the kitten, take time to consider what kind of cat will best suit your lifestyle. For example, if you have little time to spare on the cat's daily grooming, a long-haired Persian cat is not the ideal choice. Likewise, there are issues of temperament to be considered—yours as well as the cat's! Your answers to the following questions will help you come up with a good match.

WHY DO YOU WANT A CAT?

Do you want a cat for personal companionship or to provide company for another cat, or both? An active playful kitten or a sedate and affectionate adult cat? A "mouser" who will keep rodents under control or a pedigreed cat you can enter in cat shows?

Think about the kind of personality you would like in the cat, and also about the time and attention you have to give to a new pet.

Is everyone in the family ready to accept a kitten into the home?

DO YOU HAVE ROOM FOR A CAT IN YOUR HOUSE?

You will need to have ample room for a kitten to play, and a suitable place for the litter box.

WILL THE CAT SPEND TIME OUTDOORS?

Many organizations, including the Humane Society of the United States and the Cat Fanciers' Association, recommend that cats be kept indoors for their safety. Not all owners wish to follow this advice, however, and if you do intend to let your cat outdoors, please consider the following: Can you keep your kitten safe from neighbor's pets and wildlife? How will you keep the cat safe from cars in your driveway or on nearby streets?

The potential heartbreak of losing your kitten may convince you to restrict his access to the outdoors. Many owners use a leash or harness to supervise their cat's time outside. Others create an enclosed pen or garden area where the cat may enjoy the outdoors safely. Indoor and outdoor issues are covered in more detail in Chapter 3.

WILL THE KITTEN BE ALONE ALL DAY?

If no one is home during the day, consider getting two kittens to keep each other company. Cats that are bored tend to get in trouble; having a companion may reduce the mischief.

CAN YOU AFFORD VETERINARY CARE?

Even healthy kittens need occasional trips to the vet for vaccinations and an annual check-up. Can you afford the cost of spaying or neutering your pet? What about more serious medical treatment if it's needed? You may want to investigate pet insurance to help cover the cost of medical emergencies.

WHO WILL CARE FOR THE CAT WHEN YOU'RE OUT OF TOWN?
Is there a friend or neighbor who can care for the cat in your home while you're on vacation? If not, you'll need to budget for the cost of boarding your pet at a kennel while you're away.

DO YOU HAVE OTHER ANIMALS?
If so, try and ensure that your kitten comes from an environment where he has already encountered other cats and dogs. Also, consider whether the animals you already have will adjust well to the addition of a new pet.

DO YOU HAVE OR PLAN TO HAVE CHILDREN?
Animal shelters often receive cats from families who have a new baby and no longer have the time or inclination to care for their pets. Consider this carefully before you bring home a new pet: Will it still be a loved and cared-for member of the family when a baby arrives?

DO YOU NEED TO LIVE IN AN IMMACULATE HOUSE?
Even the cleanest cats shed hair, and even the best-tempered may occasionally scratch the furniture (or miss the litter box while training). What is your tolerance for accidents and messes? Will you be furious if you find a flea in the house?

DO YOU TRAVEL FREQUENTLY?
If you are a frequent traveler, consider carefully whether you can cope with a kitten. Cats like routine and can develop behavior problems if their routines are disrupted. Likewise, you will have to make plans for boarding the cat or having a friend care for it whenever you're away.

DO YOU HAVE TIME TO CARE FOR A CAT?
Are you sure you have enough free time to care for your cat, groom him and train him, and provide the attention and stimulation he needs?

WILL YOU ENJOY GROOMING YOUR NEW PET?
Not everyone enjoys—or has time for—daily pet grooming. If you don't, opt for a shorthair cat.

Finding a Pedigree Kitten

Deciding whether to get a pedigree (also known as a "purebred") or a non-pedigree cat (also known as a "domestic") depends on personal taste and budget. Pedigree cats can be quite expensive, and you may have to look outside your local area to locate a kitten of a particular breed. The benefits of buying a pedigree are that you will know what the cat will look like as an adult and what the general temperament, strengths, and weaknesses are for that breed. By buying from a reputable breeder, you can also assume your kitten has had a good start in life and comes from parents who were healthy and disease-free. The kitten should have been correctly weaned and had its first vaccinations before coming home with you.

A chinchilla Persian

Do your homework before investing in a pedigree cat.

Do your research before buying a pedigree cat to avoid costly and potentially heartbreaking mistakes. The Internet makes it easier than ever to research breeds and get advice from reputable organizations such as the Cat Fanciers' Association (http://www.cfainc.org). If there are cat shows in your area, you can see examples of numerous breeds right there in one place and ask questions of owners and breeders. There are also a number of clubs and websites dedicated to particular breeds—an Internet search will quickly lead you to them.

BUYER BEWARE

Never buy a pedigree cat without receiving a vaccination certificate, a pedigree that goes back at least four generations, a transfer of ownership form, and a diet sheet.

Acquiring a Non-Pedigree Kitten

You should not have to travel far, or pay very much, for a non-pedigree cat. Many animal shelters and rescue organizations ask only for a donation, or will even give the kitten to you in return for assurance of a good home. Be prepared to answer questions about your home and lifestyle, however, as these organizations are usually very particular about the homes their kittens go to. These days many shelters spay or neuter cats before adopting them out, and you may be required to pay a fee to cover that. In other cases, you will be asked to sign an agreement promising to have the animal neutered when it is old enough.

Many cats and kittens are "looking for good homes" as you'll see in the numerous ads placed in your newspaper by individual owners and shelters. There may also be advertisements for cats and kittens on bulletin boards in local stores, especially pet stores and animal hospitals.

When you view one of these animals, ask questions to learn as much as possible about the cat's background. If possible, view the parents to get an idea of how your kitten will look when fully grown. Unfortunately, there is often little history available about the cats and kittens awaiting homes in animal shelters.

Is a pedigree cat necessary for your family? If not, choose from the many non-pedigreed animals available in your community.

Selecting a Kitten

The kitten you choose should look happy, healthy and lively. Pick her up by cupping one hand under her chest and using the other hand to support her rear end. Lift her gently and bring her close to your body. Now check the following:

EYES:
Should be clear and free of discharge, soreness, or reddened eyelids. Healthy cats should show no sign of a gray-colored third eyelid.

NOSE AND EARS:
Must be clean and free of discharge.

COAT:
Should be clean and not greasy, without excessive dandruff. Check for little black specks which could be evidence of fleas.

BOTTOM:
Should be clean. A soiled bottom can indicate an infection.

HIGH-MAINTENANCE CATS & LOW-MAINTENANCE CATS

- Longhair and semi-longhair cats are high-maintenance. They need daily grooming and enjoy their creature comforts, often developing from fairly playful kittens into very placid adult cats.

- Shorthair cats are lower-maintenance and need significantly less grooming.

- Oriental cats, such as Siamese, are very intelligent but can be quite demanding of your attention.

- Deciding whether to get a male or female kitten is a matter of personal preference. Neither is particularly more high-maintenance, if the cat is neutered. The main difference between the sexes is that male cats tend to be larger.

All members of the litter should be bright, alert, and active.

The Formative Early Weeks

Research into animal behavior has shown that the first seven weeks of a kitten's life are the most formative ones in terms of his ability to socialize with humans.

Kittens kept in isolation during this period are likely to be less trusting and affectionate with humans later on, so try to buy a kitten from a loving family home where he has been handled frequently, has encountered other animals, and is used to things like vacuum cleaners and televisions.

If possible, arrange to see the kitten at six weeks old while it is still with the mother and other kittens. At all costs avoid buying from breeders who keep the queens (females) and kittens isolated in outdoor pens.

At about 8–12 weeks old, when the kitten is fully weaned and has had his vaccinations, he'll be ready to come home with you. Do not take the kitten home if he hates being handled or appears sickly, unless you can get written assurance from the seller that you can return the kitten and get a refund on your money if the animal does not settle or is ill.

Responsible breeders will be eager to ensure that their kitten goes to a good home, so do not be afraid to ask questions.

2

PREPARING FOR YOUR NEW KITTEN

Supplies

You'll need to stock up on a few essential items before bringing your new kitten home.

KITTEN FOOD
Try to buy the same food that your kitten ate at its previous home.

FOOD AND WATER BOWLS
Stainless steel bowls are recommended since bacteria can hide in the scratches that develop on plastic and ceramic dishes. Later you may want to invest in fancier food dishes or an automatic feeder.

WELCOME HOME!
Your kitten will make an easier transition if he has lots of attention during the first few days in his new home. Try to bring your new pet home at the start of a weekend or during a holiday break when you will have plenty of time to spend with him. If you are due to go away on vacation soon after bringing your kitten home, or if there is going to be a period of upheaval in the home (a family party, redecorating or renovation, etc.), consider postponing the kitten's arrival until things have settled down.

A cardboard box with towels or a blanket for bedding makes an ideal first bed for your kitten.

BED
A cardboard box and a blanket will do just fine, though you may want to treat your pet to a better bed at a later time.

CAT CARRIER
You will need a pet carrier for your kitten to travel home in and for trips to the vet and other journeys.

LITTER BOX AND CAT LITTER
Some cats enjoy the privacy of a covered litter box, but a simple plastic litter box usually suffices as long as it is cleaned daily. Depending on your tolerance for cleaning the litter box, you may want to consider the many varieties of "self-cleaning" types now available.

FLEA COMB AND GROOMING BRUSHES
See Chapter 3 for details on grooming supplies.

TOYS
Often the simplest toys are best. Kittens love ping-pong balls, toy mice, and cardboard boxes with holes in them. Balls and other toys stuffed with catnip are also favorites. Never leave kittens unsupervised with toys that include strings or elastic, as a kitten can become entangled and even choke himself.

SCRATCHING POST

Cats need something to scratch on in order to keep their claws clean and healthy and to prevent overgrowing. Sharpening his claws also enables your cat to leave a scent mark from his foot pads to alert other cats that he is around. Help your cat follow his instincts in this regard (and protect your furniture and belongings) by providing a scratching post. Many varieties are available in pet stores, or you can make one by wrapping a piece of carpet round a heavy wooden post. Once you have positioned the post in your home, leave it in the same place. Cats do not like their regular scratching areas to be moved.

Scratching is not just natural for cats—it's necessary.

Safety in the Home

Is your home a safe place for an inquisitive kitten to explore? Do a careful search for things that might be harmful to a curious kitten, or which the kitten might damage. Put away fragile decorative objects and small items that are easily swallowed, such as rubber bands, thumbtacks, and sewing needles. Wrap electrical cables in tape, in particular those trailing behind your television or stereo system. If the kitten shows a fondness for playing with the cords, try coating them with something your kitten will dislike, such as eucalyptus or lemon oil.

In the kitchen, keep cabinet doors shut and ensure that all household cleaners and other chemicals are safely stored. Kittens are attracted to the warmth of washing machines and dryers, so always keep appliance doors shut. In the bathroom, never leave a bath full of water unattended. The toilet also

Kittens love to explore. You may want to put fragile items away until the kitten is older and less adventurous.

presents a drowning hazard, so make it a rule that the toilet lid must be closed after each use. Accidental poisoning is another major risk for kittens. Store all medicines in a locked cabinet

Vaccination Status

Ask for a record of vaccinations when you purchase or adopt a kitten. Vaccinations are usually carried out when the kitten is between 9 and 12 weeks old. Allow at least 48 hours after the vaccinations before you bring your new kitten home.

Nearly all kittens receive vaccines to prevent several respiratory diseases known as "cat flu," as well as feline infectious enteritis, feline leukemia, and panleukopenia (distemper). Booster shots are required for most vaccines on a regular basis. Rabies vaccinations are usually given at 3–6 months of age and annually after that, depending on state and local requirements. Your vet may recommend other types of vaccination as well, depending on your type of cat and/or current local conditions and risk factors. See Chapter 5 for more information.

Finding a Vet

Word of mouth is often the best recommendation, so ask fellow cat owners which vet they see, and then schedule a visit to meet the vet and take a look at the facility. The location should be convenient enough for you to reach quickly in an emergency. Vet fees vary considerably, so ask for a price list of services. You may also want to ask whether payment plans are available if costly treatments ever become necessary.

Insurance

Pet owners today often purchase insurance policies to help minimize out-of-pocket costs for veterinary treatment. Most pet insurance policies provide coverage for vets' bills for illness and accidents to a defined dollar limit and up to a certain age; but they do not typically cover routine vaccinations or operations such as neutering. They usually do not cover any damage the cat may cause to property in your home. Some insurance companies do, however, offer coverage for special diets and homeopathic treatments. Obtain several estimates and compare benefits carefully before you make your choice. Check with other pet owners or your vet for recommendations.

Bringing Your Kitten Home

You will need some sort of cat carrier to bring your pet home in. While a cardboard box will do for the first trip, it is worth investing in a sturdy carrier with a secure lock to ensure that your adult cat does not escape on future trips. Never travel in a car with a loose cat—the distraction could cause a car accident.

Make your kitten's first journey as pleasant as possible so that she will not be afraid of the carrier in the future. Line the carrier with a thick layer of newspapers to absorb any urine, and include a towel or small blanket for the kitten to cling to or hide under. Place the carrier in a secure spot in the car where it will not shift or slide while you are driving. Use a seatbelt to strap it in if necessary. If the journey is very long, you may need to provide a litter box and have a supply of drinking water available.

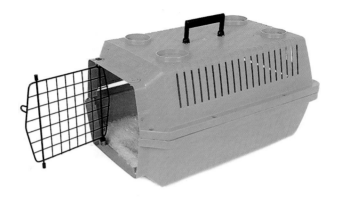

You'll need a cat carrier for bringing the kitten home as well as for trips to the vet and other traveling.

Settling In

Keep your new kitten confined to one room, with the doors and windows closed, until she settles in. Make sure you place a litter box in one corner of the room—well away from her food and water bowls, and not in a draft. Let her wander around the room in her own time, inspecting her new home, and then show your kitten her litter box and her bed, which should be away from drafts and lined with a blanket.

Your kitten will be feeling a little scared after her journey and traumatized at leaving her mother and siblings, so reassure her by talking gently and giving her plenty of cuddles. Offer her a little food, and stay with her until she begins to get tired.

Your new kitten will spend a lot of time sleeping—in fact, cats spend almost two-thirds of their lives snoozing. Encourage other family members, especially children, to respect your kitten's need to sleep.

INTRODUCE THE CAT TO YOUR NEIGHBORS.
Show your new pet to your neighbors so they know
what he looks like and can return him to you
if he ever wanders away from home.

CARING FOR YOUR CAT

Once your kitten has settled into his new home, you can turn your attention to providing the correct diet, training, exercise and grooming as he grows into adulthood.

Feeding Your Kitten

Kittens at eight weeks of age need four small meals per day. A good quality kitten food is recommended since adult cat food can be too rich for small stomachs to handle. A heaping tea-spoonful of wet kitten food will be adequate at first, but kittens grow extraordinarily fast and have very high energy

Routine feeding schedules help prevent problems related to overfeeding.

requirements so you will soon be increasing this. If the kitten cries for more to eat, offer larger portions, but be careful not to overfeed as this can cause stomach upset and diarrhea.

TYPES OF FOOD

Cats evolved as hunters and require a meat-based diet. Unlike other species such as dogs, cats do not thrive on vegetable-based diets. They simply can't synthesize the nutrients they need if deprived of meat.

Cat food and kitten food are available in many varieties. Make sure that whatever type you choose is nutritionally complete and appropriate for the age and health status of the cat. Dry food can be less costly than moist foods and has the added advantage of helping to reduce the plaque and tartar that builds up on a cat's teeth. Dry cat food can also be left out in the dish for longer periods if your kitten tends to return at a later time to finish his meal. Moist food, especially in warm rooms, will spoil fairly quickly and is likely to attract flies and other insects.

MILK

Opinions vary as to whether kittens require milk feedings after they have been weaned off their mother's milk. You can offer two small saucers of diluted milk per day, but be advised that diarrhea is fairly common in kittens drinking cow milk. You may have better results using a suitable milk-substitute available from a pet store. Consult your vet for recommendations.

WATER

A constant supply of available fresh water is essential and should be changed at least once a day. Cats eating a diet of primarily moist food require less water than do those eating mostly dry cat food.

Cats drink small quantities of water; but make sure a supply is always available.

Some cats are attracted to dripping faucets and will go to great lengths to position themselves underneath one to catch any falling drops. Others enjoy drinking from puddles or streams. Some cats will not drink tap water, but will accept filtered or bottled water.

FEEDING SCHEDULES

Stick to a routine when feeding your kitten, with meals spaced evenly throughout the day (7 AM, 1 PM, 6 PM and 10 PM, for example). A midday meal is essential for a growing kitten, so if you are not able to get home to feed him, try to arrange for a neighbor or friend to do it. Automatic feeders are another possibility for providing fresh food when you're not there to do it. Continue to feed four meals a day until the kitten is six months old. Then you can gradually change over to a two-meal per day schedule, omitting the midday meal and the late evening one.

WHAT TO DO IF YOUR CAT IS DEHYDRATED...

If you are worried that your cat is dehydrated, perhaps because he was accidentally shut in a hot building without access to water, seek immediate veterinary advice. Signs of dehydration include weakness and lethargy, intense thirst, sunken eyes, dry gums, and lack of elasticity in the skin. Severe dehydration leads to lack of coordination and collapse.

Feeding Adult Cats

Adult cats require fewer calories than kittens do, since their
growth rate and energy needs decrease over time. However, it
is still important to make sure you're offering a good quality,
nutritionally complete food. A "complete" food contains all of
the nutrients your cat requires, and you need to feed nothing
else except fresh water. There are special recipes of cat food
designed to maintain the health of older cats and there are
"lite" foods with lower fat content and fewer calories for overweight cats. Your vet can make specific recommendations to
suit your pet's particular dietary needs and should be consulted
before changing your cat's diet.

While your cat may enjoy a piece of cooked fish or chicken as
an occasional treat, feeding these regularly may encourage him
to become finicky and even refuse his regular cat food.

If your cat suffers from diarrhea or vomiting, your vet may
recommend a bland diet to control his symptoms. This may
include white meat or fish, together with white rice, and would
require eliminating cow milk from the cat's diet.

Vitamin supplements are rarely necessary. Too much of some
vitamins can be very harmful, so do not add any supplements
to your cat's diet unless directed to do so by your vet.

House Training

Cats are naturally very clean and most are fully house-trained
when they leave their mothers, so in most cases all you need to
do is show your new kitten where his litter box is. If possible,
use the same kind of cat litter the kitten is used to. Each time
he wakes up, take him to the litter box until he becomes accustomed to the new arrangements and goes there on his own.

If your kitten does not readily adjust to using the litter box, some simple changes may be effective. Try moving the litter box to a different location—the kitten may be objecting because it is too close to the feeding area or in a high traffic area such as a busy hallway. Sometimes cats do not like the type of litter in the box, so changing to a different type or brand may provide a simple solution. How often you clean—or don't clean—the litter box can also be an issue. If you clean the litter box too thoroughly and too often, you may be removing the faint traces of the smell of urine which remind the cat to use that location for toileting. On the other hand, a cat may also refuse to use a litter box because it is too dirty. If none of these factors seems to be the problem, consider keeping the cat and the litter box in a small room, such as a bathroom, for a few days to re-establish the proper toilet training habits.

Never punish your kitten if she has an accident, but be sure to clean the area thoroughly to discourage her from returning to use that spot again. Wash the soiled area thoroughly with a solution of detergent and warm water. Many commercial products are specially designed for pet stains and do a good job at removing the residual odors as well as the stains. (Remember to do a spot test on a hidden area of your carpet or upholstery before using a new cleaning product!) Never use a cleaning product which contains ammonia or chlorine, both of which are components of cat urine, or the cat may be confused because the cleaned area smells like her litter box.

You may want to place a small dish of food near the spot where the accident occurred—cats do not want to soil the areas which they associate with eating. This can deter future accidents in that location.

Exercise and Playtime

Healthy, happy kittens love to play, especially at games that simulate their hunting instincts. Be careful, however, that play does not become too rough. Even a small kitten's claws and teeth can accidentally draw blood, so stop the game and say "No" immediately when play becomes too lively. Behavior that is charming and fun in a kitten can be much less desirable in a full-grown cat.

Avoid toys which have small pieces, such as bells, that can be broken off and swallowed. Fishing-pole type toys are very popular with cats and you can purchase these or make your own from sticks, string and paper. However, toys with strings should only be used when you are there to supervise, because severe digestive problems can occur if the cat eats the string. Ribbons and yarn should be avoided for the same reason.

Some kittens can be trained to retrieve a toy in much the same way as a dog will bring a ball back to his owner. The secret in training a cat to do anything is to combine a great deal of patience with a large supply of favorite food treats such as small pieces of chicken, fish, or even cheese. Throw the toy for your kitten and, as soon as he brings it back to you, offer a food treat. Cats are ruled by their stomachs and will soon catch on to the idea that retrieving means food!

Your cat's hunting instincts will be obvious during your play times together.

The importance of grooming should not be underestimated —particularly if you have a longhair cat.

Regular Grooming

Grooming is essential to keep the coat clean and untangled. It also helps remove dead skin cells and improve circulation. While cats do spend a great deal of time grooming themselves, they cannot reach everywhere. Daily grooming also gives you the opportunity to check for health problems and to build a closer relationship with your new kitten. The amount of time you need to spend on grooming depends primarily on the length of your kitten's coat. Shorthair cats require a thorough grooming once a week, semi-longhairs need two or three sessions a week, and longhair cats should be groomed every day.

Getting your kitten used to the grooming process as early as possible is key. The secret to successful grooming is to make the whole experience as enjoyable for the cat as possible, so act confidently, keep calm, and talk to him constantly. Work for a maximum of 30 minutes at a time with frequent breaks. Do the grooming at set times so it becomes part of the cat's expected routine. Do not try to physically restrain a struggling cat—you will always get the worst of it!

Some items of equipment are essential, while others are simply nice to have. Your grooming equipment might include:

- Flea comb and metal comb (essential)

- Soft brush and slicker brush (essential)

- Small bowl filled with lukewarm water (essential)

- Cotton balls (essential)

Flea comb

- Box of soft tissues (essential)

- Towel (essential)

- Tooth-cleaning products (essential)

- Piece of chamois leather or a grooming mitt (optional)

Slicker brush

- Claw-clippers (nice to have if you are confident enough to use them)

- Baby oil (optional)

- Round-ended scissors (optional)

- Unscented talcum powder (optional)

Metal comb

Before you start, gather all your grooming tools close at hand.

Sit the kitten on your knee and spend time petting him until he is relaxed and happy. As you hold him, examine his teeth, eyes, ears, and mouth for any evidence of discharge, bad odor, or any other changes which might require the vet's attention.

Check the claws, but do not clip them unless you have first learned how to do this from your vet or a professional groomer. Always use claw-clippers and cut straight across the white tip at the end of the claw. Never cut into the pink quick, as this causes bleeding and discomfort.

Trim away any long fur around the feet using a pair of round-ended scissors. This helps keep the feet clean and tidy, and prevents cat litter from lodging between the toes.

Grooming, Step-by-Step

1. Gently wipe each eye using a moist cotton ball or cat eye-wipe. Always wipe from the inside corner of the eye to the outside. Use a new cotton ball or wipe for each eye so that you won't spread germs from one eye to the other. Tear stains can be wiped away with a commercial tear-stain remover or a warm, very weak saline solution (one level teaspoonful of salt per pint of water is sufficient).

2. Comb thoroughly, from the head to the tail, using a comb with wide-spaced teeth. Pay extra attention to the area under the chin and other hard-for-the-cat-to-reach areas. For longhair cats, comb the fur into sections and work on each section separately, gently teasing out any knots using your fingers. While you're combing, check for black specks which might indicate a flea problem.

4. Sprinkling longhair cats with talcum powder or a dry shampoo (available from pet stores) once a week will make it easier to brush out matted areas.

5. Change to a slicker brush for longhair cats, or a rubber brush or grooming mitt for shorthairs, and brush again to remove remaining dead hairs.

6. You can apply a few drops of conditioner or baby oil to your shorthair cat's coat every few weeks. This will help remove grease and improve the shine and color.

7. For a final "polish," wipe the cat down with a piece of chamois leather.

CARING

Hold your kitten gently but firmly and he will soon accept the grooming routine. Talk to him while you groom him and make grooming a pleasant experience for both of you.

This well-trained Persian cat sits quietly for grooming, even when younger members of the family help.

DOES YOUR CAT HATE TO BE GROOMED?

Dislike of grooming usually occurs as a result of pain, such as someone being rough when removing tangles from the cat's coat. It's also possible that a medical problem, such as skin irritation or a developing abscess, is the reason the cat does not want to be groomed—consult your vet.

Resolve to make the grooming experience as pleasant as possible. Be prepared to be very patient. Breaking the grooming down into small components will help. Begin by, literally, just laying a brush on the cat's coat, then quickly removing it and giving the cat a food treat as a reward. Do not put pressure on him by grooming for too long at any one session. A few minutes of successful grooming is better than an hour-long session ending with an angry cat and a frustrated owner.

Molting (Shedding) and Hair-Balls

Outdoor cats generally molt (shed) in spring and autumn, but indoor cats, living in centrally heated homes, can appear to be shedding most of the time.

Hair-shedding is a natural process, but very heavy hair loss at unexpected times can be a sign of illness. Contact your vet for advice if this appears to be a problem.

From time to time a cat may cough up or pass hair-balls. These consist of hair ingested by the cat during grooming. Hair tends to ball up in the stomach, forming a tight mass. It can be quite alarming when your cat appears to be vomiting or retching in order to rid himself of these hair-balls, but the cat generally handles this without any need for intervention on your part. However, if he appears extremely distressed, has prolonged choking, or is extremely constipated, contact a vet.

The best way to minimize the formation of hair-balls, and to prevent the accumulation of loose hair on your furniture and clothes, is to groom regularly. There are also cat food varieties available which help to reduce the build-up of hair-balls in a cat's stomach.

Bathing

It is rarely necessary to bathe a shorthair cat, but longhair cats benefit from a monthly bath. Bathing should always be done after the cat has been thoroughly combed, otherwise tangles will "set" when dry and be impossible to brush out.

Get everything you need ready first so that you will not need to take your attention away from the cat once you start bathing her. If you wash your cat in the sink or bath, place a rubber mat in the bottom to give her something to grip. The temperature of the water should be comfortable, neither too hot or too cold. Avoid getting water into the cat's eyes or ears.

A cat that is anxious about being in the water may accept standing on a dry surface and being gently rinsed with a hose. Use a shampoo that is specifically designed for cats (not for other types of small animals) and be sure to rinse thoroughly. Wrap the cat in a towel afterward and dry off the excess water. Some owners dry the cat further with a hair dryer on a low setting but this often requires the help of a second person.

Dental Care

According to a survey on cat health by the University of Kansas, an amazing 85 percent of cats over the age of three years old suffer from periodontal problems, and some cats develop tooth and gum problems at a much younger age.

These diseases damage not just teeth and gums but, left untreated, can be life-threatening if the infection spreads to other parts of the body.

Feeding your cat a diet consisting primarily of dry food is an important part of preventing these problems. The texture of dry food helps reduce plaque and tartar build-up.

Make it a habit right from the start to brush your kitten's teeth on a daily basis. Many cats learn to find this process soothing and even enjoyable. There are lots of cat dental care products on the market, including toothpaste and brushes or teeth-cleaning wipes, pads, and solutions. Place a blob of cat toothpaste on your finger and let him sniff it and lick it before you begin. Hold your cat from behind, then lift her chin and gently rub the teeth using either a soft brush or your finger. Clean a couple of teeth the first few times and, as he accepts this, gradually do a few more.

Your vet should do a thorough check of the cat's mouth and teeth at least once a year.

Take photos of your kitten throughout her life. Her appearance will change as she grows, especially during the first year. These photos will also be helpful for making fliers should your pet go missing.

FAMILY LIFE WITH CATS

Scientific evidence shows that children who own pets are less self-centered and more outgoing than those who do not. There is also some indication that pet ownership can increase the attention span of children with learning difficulties, and studies of abused children reveal that pets can offer a strong supportive role during times of upheaval, such as divorce or family illness. Owning a cat certainly helps teach children valuable lessons about responsibility and respecting other living creatures.

With a few ground rules and careful supervision, children and kittens will be the best of friends and playmates.

Understanding Your Cat

HOW CATS SEE:
Because cats are hunters, their senses are highly tuned. Cats' eyes are designed to give them optimum vision during their most active periods: sunset and dawn. Their night vision is very effective, perhaps eight times more so than ours. However, they see fewer colors than we do and cannot differentiate between reds, which probably look gray or black to them. They can make out shades of blue or green but are much more interested in the shape of an object and its movement than its color.

HOW CATS HEAR:
Cats also hear better than we do, especially ultrasonic, high-pitched noises. The extremely sensitive pads on their feet enable them to detect ground vibrations, a trait which is especially helpful when hunting. You will notice that your kitten often puts his head to one side when he is listening to something—this is his way of working out which direction a noise is coming from. He will do this less frequently as he grows older and more experienced. Cats tell the direction a sound originates from by using both ears to process the noise and then comparing the received information.

HOW CATS COMMUNICATE:
Your kitten has many methods of communication; but to us humans, purring is certainly one of the nicest. Not everything is known about purring, but it is thought that the sound is produced by the cat's vocal cords vibrating together. The glottis (the gap between the chords) opens and closes up to 25 times per second and the pressure of air passing in and out results in the noise we recognize as purring. Purring occurs when the cat is happy and relaxed, and it is often used in greeting.

Purring can also occur when a cat is distressed or worried, such as during a visit to the vet. In this case it is thought to be a source of comfort and a plea for help from other cats or from the owner. It probably relates back to happier times when the kitten was snuggled up with his purring mother.

FAMILY LIFE

Ground Rules for Children

Cats vary in personality. While some are extremely tolerant with children, others become impatient quite quickly. Ideally, your kitten will have experienced some family life before coming to your home. Kittens that are already familiar with kids, vacuum cleaners, telephones, and other loud noises have a far easier time adapting to life in a busy household.

Establish some ground rules right from the start, teaching children by example how to treat the kitten with respect and affection. Show them how to treat the kitten gently and lovingly, explaining that loud noises can be very frightening, as can sudden movements, or grabbing at the kitten's ears, whiskers or tail. Emphasize that your new kitten is not a toy and cannot be squeezed, chewed, or handled like a rag doll. Also teach them not to touch the kitten while he is sleeping or eating.

Older children can be taught to observe the cat's behavior and apply some judgement as to whether he is contented or not. Point out that signs of displeasure include ruffling of the fur and hissing or flattening of the ears, while signs of pleasure include purring and rubbing against the legs.

Involving children in caring for the kitten will help develop a sense of mutual respect. Asking the child to help you feed the kitten will enable the kitten to begin associating the child with positive events.

Good hygiene is vital. Keep the cat's food bowls and litter box well away from children and ensure that the cat does not have access to your child's dishes. Cat food should also be kept separate from human foods. Teach children to wash their hands after playing with the cat, especially before meal times. Be careful not to leave uneaten cat food around for too long as it may attract both flies and toddlers!

TAKE PRECAUTIONS AGAINST POISONING
Store any animal medications, worming powders, etc.
in a secure place, well out of reach of children and pets.
The same is true for human medications as well as household
cleaners and other chemicals—store them safely!

The Growing Family

PREGNANCY

Pregnant women are often concerned about an infection called toxoplasmosis, which can be passed from cats to humans and cause harm to the eyes or brain of a developing fetus. *Toxoplasma* is a single-celled parasite found in almost all mammals, but cats are significant in its life-cycle. Cats rarely show signs of the illness so you won't be able to tell if they are infected. They only spread *Toxoplasma* in their feces for a few weeks after being infected.

The good news is that fastidious hygiene minimizes the risk of any possible infection, so there is no need to get rid of your cat when you find out you're pregnant. The Centers for Disease Control (CDC) recommend that, if you are pregnant, you have someone else clean the litter box on a daily basis. If no one else can do it for you, wear plastic gloves and wash your hands thoroughly with soap and water immediately afterward.

Cats who roam (and eat) outdoors are much more likely to ingest the parasite than cats kept indoors. The way that a cat —or a person—can get toxoplasmosis is by eating raw or undercooked meat which contains the parasite. If you are pregnant, follow your doctor's recommendations concerning safe handling of raw meat. Keep your cat indoors and avoid other cats, especially strays, who roam outdoors.

Consult your doctor and your vet for additional advice.

CATS AND BABIES

There are many superstitions and "urban legends" concerning cats harming babies, but there is little proof to back them up. In particular, people may tell you that cats can smother babies or suffocate them by "sucking the air" out of a baby's mouth.

Cats enjoy sleeping in warm places and have probably been blamed for infant deaths due to SIDS and other causes simply because they were seen in the baby's room. The smell of milk on a baby's breath may also attract cats to come close and try to lick their faces. Most experts today would tell you that it is wise to keep your cat out of the baby's room, and especially out of the baby's bed, but for several more practical reasons.

FAMILY LIFE

You don't want the cat to scare the baby or to scratch it accidentally. You also don't want the cat to sleep close to the baby's face, just as you don't want the baby to have its face pressed into the fur of a stuffed animal. Anything that impairs the baby's breathing is—obviously—to be avoided.

As with any other pet, you'll want to supervise your cat when it is near the baby. Establish early on that the baby's room is off-limits, especially the crib or bed. Keep the door to that room shut and you won't have to wonder whether the cat is in there when you put the baby down to sleep.

Some people also choose to buy a crib net, a piece of mesh fabric that attaches to the crib, in order to keep a toddler from trying
to climb out. These can be used to keep cats from climbing in, but you should make sure that the crib net is held taut so that it will not encourage a cat to use it as a comfy hammock.

DON'T YOU LOVE ME ANYMORE?
Cats, especially older ones, can perceive the arrival of a baby in the house as threatening. With the baby comes a host of new smells and sounds, and a big decrease in human attention paid to the cat. Being exposed to other babies in advance can help the cat adapt to the family's new child.

Though a new baby means big changes for everyone, do make an effort to pay attention to your pets as they adjust to the new arrival. Behavioral problems may occur during transitions, so try to be patient and understanding if your cat develops a temporary tendency to scratch the furniture or miss the litter box.

Coping with Cat Allergies
It can be very distressing to discover that a child or family member is allergic to your new cat. Coughing, sneezing, and runny eyes are just some of the uncomfortable symptoms that allergy sufferers have to contend with. Medication such as antihistamines, or even steroids, may be necessary to alleviate these symptoms.

If anyone in your household has a known allergy to animals, or has asthma, consider this carefully before bringing home a new pet that you might not be able to keep.

Some allergy sufferers react to cat dander, the skin particles routinely shed by cats, while others react to a substance which is secreted from the sebaceous glands of the cat's skin. Once these substances become airborne, they can be inhaled into the lungs or picked up on the skin, causing an allergic reaction.

Rigorous house cleaning may help reduce the sources of allergy symptoms. Dust regularly with a damp cloth, regularly wash curtains and soft furnishings, and air the house thoroughly by opening the windows. Vacuuming, while necessary, tends to make dander particles airborne and more problematic for allergy sufferers. Do not vacuum while allergy sufferers are nearby in the house or right before they come to visit. Your family doctor or allergist can provide advice on treatment options.

Defining "Off-Limits" Areas

Decide which areas of your house are off-limits to the cat and be consistent right from the start in training him where he is not welcome. Teach him that he is not allowed in the baby's room, for example, and that he should not jump onto kitchen work surfaces. Other problem areas for kittens include laundry machines (a cat can get trapped inside), bathtubs, and baby cribs and carriages. Begin early in reinforcing that the kitten is not allowed in these areas.

A plastic spray bottle filled with water or a small water-pistol can be useful in training your cat to stay away from forbidden areas. If the cat jumps onto the kitchen counter, for example, immediately say a loud "No" and then aim a well-directed squirt from the spray bottle. Cats dislike being sprayed with water and will soon get the message that work surfaces are not attractive places to explore. Eventually, simply saying the word "No," without spraying him with water, should be sufficient. Cats also dislike the feel of aluminum foil under their paws, so covering surfaces with this will help discourage him from walking on those areas when you are not around.

Kittens and Other Pets

Successfully introducing a kitten into a multi-pet household is usually easier than bringing in an older cat. The key to success is never to force the issue. Take your time to introduce the animals to each other in a gradual way.

In the wild, cats recognize newcomers by their smell. Learning to accept this smell as non-threatening is the first step to getting your pets to accept a newcomer. You can help this process by keeping your kitten or new cat in a separate room of the house for the first day or two. This way, although the newcomer is out of sight, very subtle scent signals, unnoticed by humans, will begin to infiltrate the house.

After a day or two, try a face-to-face introduction between the new kitten and an older cat or dog. The best way to do this is by using a large cage or pet carrier. The carrier should be big enough to contain a bed, a litter box, food and water. Put your new kitten or cat into the carrier and allow your other pet to wander up and sniff him. Do not worry if there is lots of hissing or growling—your kitten will be safe inside.

The two animals will gradually accept the fact that they can see and smell each other without threat or fear of attack. Short but frequent "introduction" periods allow the animals to get

A carrier can be used to help your other pets accept your new kitten.

Feeding the pets together is very helpful during the transition. Build up to this gradually, first with the kitten in a pen or carrier.

used to each other. In the meantime, keep the animals separate and give each of them plenty of individual attention. If the other pet goes outside during the day, use this time to allow your new kitten to explore the rest of the house, thus distributing his scent even further.

The next stage is to begin feeding the animals together. Feed your kitten in her carrier and place a food bowl for the other pet nearby. You can reverse this arrangement for the next meal so that the older cat or dog eats his meal inside the carrier and the kitten eats outside. Food helps animals relax with each other and reinforces the message that the kitten is not a threat.

When the animals seem happy, you can forgo the carrier, but resist the temptation to grab the kitten or shout at the other pet if problems arise. Being over-protective of the kitten could make your other pet jealous and this would be counter-productive. When introducing other pets to your kitten always ensure that there are escape routes available so the kitten can hide if she needs to.

The best way to help your kitten make new friends is to take things slowly and approach introductions from the point of view of the animals rather than humans.

Your kitten will soon learn to let sleeping dogs lie.

WHY CAN'T THEY JUST GET ALONG?

What do you do when cats who have lived together in harmony for several years suddenly become aggressive toward each other? Often the reason for a rift between cats is a subtle change in the cat's scent, perhaps because of a trip to the vet or groomer's, etc. Resist the temptation to shout at the aggressive cat and rush to protect the "victim" as this will only perpetuate the problem. Instead, try feeding the aggressive cat or giving him a treat when the other cat is present so that pleasant associations begin to re-establish themselves.

In extreme cases, you may have to reintroduce the cats to each other as if they were strangers, getting them to accept each other's scent. Keep the cats separate and provide each one with a towel or blanket to sleep on. Every night alternate the towels so that they get used to each other's scent. After a couple of weeks, reintroduce the cats by confining one of them to an indoor pen and allowing them to sniff each other in safety. Next day, reverse the situation and keep the other one confined. With patience and time, the cats should, once again, begin to accept each other, but there are no guarantees. In some cases, only a permanent separation resolves the situation.

*Fish-watching is a fascinating pastime for a kitten. The fish
will come to no harm, as long as the tank has a secure lid.
However...*

*...bird-watching is potentially more hazardous. Never leave
your kitten alone with birds or small animals.*

Indoor Cats

Many owners decide to keep their cats indoors to keep them safe from cars, other animals (both wild and domestic), poisonous plants, and other hazards. Organizations like the Humane Society of the United States (HSUS) and the Cat Fanciers' Association (CFA) strongly recommend that pet cats be kept indoors. Some shelters and pet adoption centers require that prospective owners agree to this before taking home a pet.

If you decide to keep your cat indoors, you must provide him with sufficient exercise and stimulation to keep him active and fit. This will also reduce the likelihood of destructive behaviors such as clawing at furniture or soiling in inappropriate places. Owners who work all day may want to consider getting two kittens to provide each other with company and entertainment, thus reducing the potential for mischief.

Ensure that your indoor cat has plenty of opportunities to climb, play, explore, and sunbathe. Scratching posts are essential for making sure that cats work their nails in an approved location rather than on your furniture or other household items. Climbing frames are also fun for your cats and provide plenty of exercise.

If you decide that your cat will spend time outdoors, it is essential that you take precautions to keep her safe.

Venturing Outside

When your kitten has had her vaccinations and is thoroughly settled in her new home, you may decide it is time to let her explore the world outside. Be guided in your decision by considering your environment, the cat's temperament, and her health status.

Purchase a collar for your outdoor cat which is reflective (to help reduce chance of being hit by a car at night) and has a "breakaway" feature to ensure that it will snap under tension rather than cutting off the cat's breathing if she gets caught on something.

Proper identification is essential. Identification tags with your name and phone number are a good start, but are not much help if the cat's collar is removed or lost. Many pet owners opt to get a microchip implanted under the cat's skin for identification. This procedure is carried out by a vet and involves the painless insertion of a tiny chip (about the size of a grain of rice) under the skin. It is usually done in the neck area where it remains in place for the rest of the cat's life. Should the cat become lost and be picked up by the local animal control department, or taken to a vet in the case of an accident, a scanner will reveal the number of the microchip and the cat can be readily reunited with her owner. The cost of microchipping varies, but the benefits are obvious, even for indoor cats (who sometimes escape through open doors or windows).

Cat Doors

Some owners allow their cats the freedom to go in and out of the house as they please by installing a cat door. There are many cat doors on the market, ranging from simple designs to high-tech models with electronic, magnetic, infrared, or other features to keep other animals out and ensure that only your cat can enter the house. Whichever type you choose, it should be fitted about 6 inches (15 cm) from the base of the door to make it easy for the cat to step through.

Training your cat or kitten to use a cat door requires patience. Never force him through or he may reject it completely.

With time, patience, and food treats, you can teach your kitten to use a cat door.

Instead, tempt him through with cat treats and praise, particularly at meal times when he is a little hungry and more likely to respond. He will soon get the hang of it.

The Cat-Friendly Yard

Placing marker posts in corners of the yard encourages cats to scent there, and scratching posts will help protect your favorite trees from sharp claws. Ensure there are some shaded areas in the garden where your cat can escape from the heat of the day. Encourage cats to use only one area of the garden as a toilet. They will appreciate a pit of dry, sharp sand on a raised area (away from the reach of toddlers), especially if tall grasses are planted around it for privacy. Sift the sand and add new sand frequently. If your garden contains a children's sandbox you'll want to keep this covered when not in use so that your cat does not mistake it for a giant litter box.

Cats are fond of nibbling grass because it aids their digestion. They also adore plants such as catnip and cat-mint, both of which are available in seed form and can be grown very easily. Many plants, however, are poisonous to cats, including azaleas, buttercups, chrysanthemums, crocus, foxglove, hyacinths, jasmine, mistletoe, morning glory, periwinkles, tulips, winter cherry, and yew.

You will also need to take some steps to reduce the likelihood of your cat getting into a hazardous situation. Contrary to popular belief, cats and kittens are often fascinated by water, particularly the trickles produced by fountains and sprinklers. Prevent drowning by keeping water buckets and other containers covered, and try to keep the cat away from ponds or pools.

Garages and sheds are high-risk areas for cats and kittens. Try to restrict your cat's access to these buildings. Animals may become trapped inside a hot building when the door is closed by someone who doesn't know the pet is in there. Starvation and dehydration are definitely risks in such cases.

Toxic chemicals such as cleaners and anti-freeze also pose a major danger for cats. Take precautions to make sure containers are not left open or accessible to your pets. If you suspect your cat has ingested something poisonous, contact your vet immediately.

Coming When Called

It's a good idea to teach your cat to come when called, or at least to "answer" you by meowing. This will help you locate him quickly when he is outdoors. The best way to train him is by tapping a saucer with a fork as you shout his name. Cats are sensitive to high-pitched sounds and will hear this noise from quite a long distance.

Rattling a box of kitty treats is another way to encourage your cat to return when called. If you let him out before feeding time, he'll have a strong incentive—hunger—to come immediately when he hears this signal. Always offer your cat a food reward for coming when called and give him lots of praise.

Cat Runs

Constructing a "cat run" is one solution for those who want their cats to go outdoors but stay in a controlled area. Look for ads for these in cat-care magazines or contact a carpenter for a custom-built design. A building permit may be required.

Cat Harnesses

Another way to allow supervised visits outdoors is by training your kitten to accept a harness and leash. Not all cats will allow this, but a kitten that is accustomed to wearing a harness around the house will be more likely to accept a leash than an older cat being introduced to it for the first time. Oriental types such as Siamese seem particularly agreeable to being restrained in this way.

Start getting your young kitten used to the harness by letting him wear it for a few minutes each day.

Allow your kitten to sniff the harness thoroughly before you attempt to put it on so that he becomes familiar with its smell and does not perceive it as threatening.

Wearing the harness for a few minutes, two to three times each day, and receiving praise and treats, will help your kitten develop a positive attitude toward it. When the harness is accepted, you can try attaching the leash and letting the kitten get used to the feel of it. Walking calmly on the leash should be encouraged by treats and praise.

If your cat remains distressed and won't accept a harness, you may have to abandon the idea.

Behavioral Issues

Most feline behavioral problems, such as inappropriate spraying, are the result of stress and frustration. Chances are that the cat is trying to tell you something important. Here are some tips to help you deal with the most common challenges.

AGGRESSION

A cat who suddenly develops aggressive behavior may do so because she is in pain, so a thorough exam by a vet is necessary. If no medical cause is found, then the cause of the aggression may be rooted in a fear response. Perhaps a new cat has moved into the neighborhood or there has been disruption in the household such as divorce or even a wedding. Your vet will be able to offer advice on this and may refer you to an animal behaviorist for further treatment.

INDOOR SPRAYING AND SOILING

Urine spraying is normal feline behavior and is exhibited naturally by all outdoor cats. It simply becomes unacceptable to us when the cat performs the behavior indoors. Never resort to physical abuse when dealing with this type of problem—the cat has very good reasons of his own for soiling or spraying where he does.

The first step is to rule out a medical cause. Next, try to determine whether the cat is spraying or soiling to mark territory or for some other reason. You may not even know that a new cat

Patience is essential when dealing with any type of behavioral problem.

has moved into the neighborhood, but your cat will! Territory marking can also occur when the cat's security is challenged by some disruption to his routine within the home, such as renovation or decorating. A cat that is marking often sprays in certain areas but continues to use the litter box. On the other hand, cats with toileting problems often stop using the litter box completely, preferring to use a quiet, secluded place such as behind a sofa or under a bed.

Cats who do not respond to simple changes in housekeeping, such as repositioning the litter box, changing litter type, and thoroughly cleaning soiled areas, may benefit from going back to basics. Confining the cat to a small room, containing only a bed and a litter tray, for a few days may do the trick. This limits the choices of where the cat should soil and the urge not to soil in his bed will help him choose the litter box. A couple of days will be sufficient; do not confine the cat any longer.

REFUSING THE CAT CARRIER
If your cat hides whenever you get the carrier out to take her to the vet or elsewhere, leave the carrier out in the open near the cat's bed. Put toys and food treats inside it and encourage your kitten to explore by herself. Your cat will soon realize the carrier is not threatening and will be less fearful about going into it.

DESTRUCTIVE BEHAVIOR

Cats can cause a great deal of damage by scratching furniture and wallpaper, breaking items on display, or chewing and scratching a favorite rug. It is important to realize that cats are never motivated by malice toward their owners— even if they have had a particularly bad day they will never think: *I am going to knock this china teapot on the floor and really annoy someone.* They are simply amusing themselves.

Providing toys and scratching posts helps curb tendencies toward destructive behavior.

Scratching is a normal cat behavior and is essential for removing outer claw sheaths, claw-conditioning, and providing visual and scent signals to other cats. If you keep your cat indoors, provide him with a scratching post so he can perform this behavior in a place that is acceptable to you. Introducing a

DE-CLAWING: A CONTROVERSIAL TOPIC

While we understand the frustration owners feel when cats exercise their claws on furniture, carpets, and other household items, surgical de-clawing should not be considered the first or best solution. Opponents argue that this type of surgery is unethical because it is done for the owner's benefit, not the cat's, and puts the cat at risk during general anesthesia. De-clawing also negatively affects the cat's natural movement and its ability to defend itself. It may even cause changes in personality. Instead, provide scratching posts, train your cat gently and consistently to use them, and keep your cat's claws properly trimmed. If the cat continues to scratch in the wrong places, you may want to explore using "nail caps," plastic covers which are attached to the claws. Check with your vet and your pet store for more suggestions.

new kitten to the scratching post at an early age will help prevent problems from developing.

Scratching as a means of scent marking can be deterred by thorough cleaning of the area to remove all traces of the scent.

Never ignore destructive feline behavior, even in tiny kittens, as it can develop into a compulsive disorder. Try to distract your kitten from problem behaviors by playing a game with her. Keep a plastic water spray bottle handy and spray your cat, while saying a loud "No," if you catch her scratching wallpaper or furniture. Immediately take the cat to her scratching post so that she knows where she should exercise her claws.

HUNTING
Cats are natural hunters and often enjoy presenting their favorite people with a gift such as a mouse or a dead bird. Unfortunately, these gifts are not always appreciated by their owners who tend to scream and make a fuss, causing the cat much confusion! It is far more effective to respond calmly and attempt to distract him from his prey using food or a toy.

The cat is a natural hunter—and although you can limit his opportunities, you will not alter his instincts.

Putting a collar with a bell on the cat may help alert birds and other animals that your cat is on the hunt, although cats can become so adept at moving slowly that the bell does not make a noise until it is too late. Keeping your cat indoors during the prime hunting times, early morning and dusk, will help to protect the wildlife in your area.

If you put food out for birds, place it in a wide open space to give the birds an escape route and to prevent your cat from reaching them too easily.

Choosing a Boarding Kennel

There are times when you may need to leave your cat at a boarding kennel. Ask other cat owners for recommendations and visit the facility to make your own survey. Reputable kennels welcome visitors and, provided you do not arrive at a busy time of the day, will be happy to show you around so you can make an informed decision.

Check for the following:
- Is everything spotlessly clean?
- Are the cages or "condos" roomy enough? They should be at least four feet square and have about two feet between pens to reduce the risk of infection being spread.
- Are the condos well insulated, clean and painted? Is there adequate ventilation and heating?
- Do the cats look clean and well cared for? Are their litter boxes clean? What type of bedding is used? Can you take your own?
- Are you asked to produce vaccination certificates? Does the director ask for your cat's feeding history, vet's name and contact telephone numbers?
- Is fresh water available in all the pens?
- Do the condos have locking cat doors?
- Where is the food prepared? Does the kitchen area look clean and well organized?
- Does the price include everything, or are there extra costs?
- Will your cat be groomed?
- What will happen if your cat is ill during his stay?
- How much are cancellation fees and what insurance arrangements does the kennel have?

Good boarding kennels fill up very quickly during peak periods such as holidays, so plan to do your research well in advance and make your reservation as early as possible.

WHAT TO DO
IF YOUR PET IS MISSING

Take action immediately!

- Enlist the help of friends and family to make a thorough search of the area, including sheds, garages, and abandoned buildings.

- Telephone local vets to see if a cat of your cat's description has been brought in or found injured.

- Contact nearby animal shelters and animal control departments to see if your cat has been brought in.

- Make a flier, complete with a photograph of your cat and details of where and when he went missing. Distribute these to houses in your area.

- Post your flier in conspicuous places throughout the neighborhood (on trees and telephone polls, etc.) and on the bulletin boards of local shops and supermarkets.

- If your cat has a microchip for identification purposes, telephone the relevant organization to alert it to the fact that your pet is missing.

- Search the same area repeatedly, as a lost cat can take some weeks to establish himself in a new area.

5

KEEPING YOUR CAT HEALTHY

Daily Checks

- Observe your kitten and be alert to any changes in her behavior such as loss of appetite, excessive thirst, weight loss, unusual aggression or listlessness.

- Groom your kitten for a few minutes each day, especially if she is a longhair cat. This gives you the opportunity to check for obvious health problems such as fleas. As in humans, dull lifeless hair may indicate health problems.

- Check your kitten's teeth. Cleaning is not essential at a very young age because she will lose her baby teeth just before

Purring is a sign that your cat is relaxed and content.

six months, but it's good to get her used to having her mouth and gums handled. Heavy build-up of plaque on the teeth of adult cats can cause pain when eating and lead to tooth loss. This plaque can be removed under general anesthetic by a vet, but feeding some dry food, or special anti-plaque chews, each day will help prevent build-up.

- Dispose of any uneaten food the kitten leaves in her dish and thoroughly wash her food and water bowls.

- Remove any soiling from the litter tray.

Weekly Checks

- Check the eyes for signs of redness, discoloration, or discharge. There should be no sign of the third eyelid.

- Check the ears. These are normally clean and pink, though slightly waxy. Look for evidence of discharge or a foul smell. Persistent scratching or head-shaking and excess wax may indicate ear mites, while a bad smell can signal a bacterial or fungal infection.

- Check the nose and mouth. There should be no evidence of discharge or a foul smell.

- Clean and disinfect the cat's litter box, avoiding strong-smelling products which may discourage the cat from using the box. Disposable litter box liners are thrown away with the dirty litter and can make the process easier.

Monthly Checks

- Some methods of flea control are done on a monthly basis. (See **Parasite Infections** on page 57.) Write the dates on a calendar to remind you.

- Outdoor cats that are keen hunters benefit from monthly worm control. Indoor cats may only need to be wormed once or twice a year. Check with your vet for advice.

Annual Checks

- Your cat will require at least one trip to the vet each year for his vaccination boosters and annual health examination. Put a reminder in your calendar to schedule this.

- Check that your cat's health insurance is up to date.

Vaccinations

Your kitten's first vaccinations are usually carried out between the ages of 8 and 12 weeks, when the antibodies he receives from his mother have dropped to a low enough level not to interfere with the vaccine. Vaccines provide protection against some of the most serious feline diseases.

- Feline Infectious Enteritis is an extremely serious and often fatal disease, producing symptoms including dehydration, vomiting, and diarrhea. Routine vaccination has resulted in almost total control of this disease.

- Cat Flu is a common group of viral respiratory diseases (including feline herpes virus, feline calici virus, and rhino-tracheitis) which, though rarely fatal, can make your kitten very ill.

- Panleukopenia (distemper) is a life-threatening viral illness and is particularly dangerous for unvaccinated kittens. Diarrhea, vomiting, low white blood count, and seizures are the main symptoms.

- Feline Leukemia causes immunodeficiency disease and cancerous tumors in cats. Half the cats infected with this virus die within two to three years. Today's vaccine offers a high degree of protection against the disease.

ANOTHER GOOD REASON TO KEEP SHOTS UP-TO-DATE
Reputable boarding facilities will ask you to produce vaccination certification from your vet, so ensure that your cat's vaccinations are up to date five to six weeks before you plan to board him.

Your vet will be able to tell you which vaccines are necessary or recommended for your cat, and set up an appropriate schedule for booster shots.

Vaccines are now available to offer some protection against Feline Immunodeficiency Virus (FIV), sometimes referred to as the feline equivalent of the AIDS virus. This disease is NOT transmissible to humans and is not spread by sexual contact between cats but primarily via cat bites. It is most prevalent among aggressive male cats, which provides another incentive for neutering. Indoor cats are at much less risk of contracting FIV than cats that roam outdoors. Talk with your vet about the advantages and disadvantages of FIV vaccination

The Importance of Neutering

A female cat can produce up to three litters a year, with five or six kittens in each litter. Females are sexually mature at the age of six months and males are capable of fathering a litter at seven months. Consult your vet or the local Humane Society to make plans to have your kitten spayed or neutered before six months of age.

The procedures for spaying and neutering are simple and require only a short stay at the vet's. The cost varies, but your vet may offer payment options or refer you to a source of financial assistance for this purpose. Contact your local animal rescue organization or humane association to find out whether low-cost neutering is available through their programs.

People often resist neutering their pets for reasons which are based on anecdotal evidence rather than fact. One common myth is that female cats are healthier if they are not spayed until after their first litter is born, but there is a great deal of scientific evidence now which shows the opposite is true.

In addition to ending the possibility of unwanted litters and adding to the dramatic numbers of unwanted and neglected pets, neutering reduces or eliminates a variety of health problems, including uterine and ovarian cancer in females and testicular cancer in males. Neutered cats also tend to be more affectionate and less aggressive. They are less likely to stray away from home or to display destructive behavior like scratching or spraying to mark their territory.

Parasite Infections

Cats can be infected by endoparasites that live inside the body and ectoparasites that live on the surface. Roundworms, tapeworms, and lungworms are endoparasites, while fleas, ticks, lice, and mites are ectoparasites.

Worming products will rid your cat of parasites he currently has but they do not prevent acquiring more, so regular treatment is needed. Outdoor cats, particularly those who enjoy hunting, tend to be more susceptible to parasite infection than indoor cats.

Flea infestation is the most common feline problem treated by vets. Fleas love the warm, humid environment that central heating, insulated windows, and wall-to-wall carpeting provide. Adult fleas are small, brownish-colored insects with huge leg muscles enabling them to jump vast distances. They live in the coat of your cat and lay eggs which often drop to the ground, burrowing into your carpet or soft furnishings until they are big enough to hatch and jump onto the nearest cat, dog or, as a last resort, human, who happens to walk by.

Tell-tale signs of fleas are small black specks which fall off during grooming. They are more noticeable if you comb your cat while he is standing on a clean white sheet of paper. Untreated flea infestation can cause severe itching, skin irritation, and hair loss.

To prevent flea infestation:

- Comb your cat regularly with a special flea comb.

- If your cat is used to being bathed, try a flea repellent shampoo and rinse.

- Treat your cat's bedding and your home, as well as your cat.

- Vacuum your home thoroughly and have the carpets steam-cleaned if infestation is suspected.

There are many safe and highly effective flea repellents available today, including some that are only available from a vet. Some disrupt the breeding cycle of the flea by rendering them infertile after they bite the cat. These are usually available as a liquid and are administered each month by injection or by adding them to the cat's food. Other forms include collars, sprays, powders, foams or tablets. Check the labeling since some older-style products may contain organophosphate ingredients and, if used, care should be taken with their administration and disposal. They are usually too strong for use on a kitten or a cat who is nursing kittens, and many pet owners prefer to avoid products with organophosphates altogether.

Never use more than one product at a time on your cat; and if you suspect he or she has had an allergic reaction, contact your vet immediately.

"Alternative" flea repellents are also available. Unlike chemical insecticides, these do not kill the flea and will not disrupt the flea's breeding cycle. There are flea repellent collars containing herbs and essential oils, shampoos or rinses, and flea repellent oils such as lavender, rosemary, cedarwood, or lemon diluted in a carrier oil.

Some owners add a quarter-teaspoonful of cider vinegar to the cat's food, which is supposed to make the cat's blood taste repugnant to fleas. Feeding garlic supplements is another popular method of natural flea control. For more information on natural health care remedies, contact your vet.

Common Health Problems

By nature, cats are independent creatures and, when they are ill, often retreat to a quiet corner rather than acting in a way that would let you know something is obviously wrong. This is why it is important for you to pay attention to your cat's normal daily behavior and appetite so you can spot changes which may indicate a health problem.

Consult your vet regarding any of these symptoms:

- Loss of appetite or excessive thirst
- Sudden weight loss
- Skin problems such as hair loss or sore patches
- Persistent vomiting or diarrhea
- Discharge from the eyes or ears
- Breathing problems
- Abnormal behavior such as hiding or sudden aggression when touched
- Limping or inhibited movement

In an emergency, such as a road accident, cats instinctively bolt and find somewhere to hide in an effort to avoid further injury and attack by predators. By the time injured cats are found, other symptoms have often developed such as dehydration,

IS YOUR CAT TOO FAT?
Cats, just like humans, put on excess weight when they combine a sedentary lifestyle with a diet that's high in calories or fat. Also like humans, overweight cats are at greater risk for heart disease, arthritis, and other medical problems. The "ideal weight" for your cat depends on its age, gender, and breed—ask your vet for advice if you think your cat is getting too heavy.

infection and/or shock. In the event your cat is injured, telephone your veterinary office and alert them you are on your way so they will be ready when you arrive.

Poisoning, accidental or otherwise, is a big problem for cats. NEVER give your cat human medication unless directed by your vet. Aspirin and acetaminophen are highly toxic to cats—even one dose can be fatal.

Like humans, cats are affected by sun exposure and excessive heat. Outdoor cats should always have access to shade and cold water. Some cats, particularly white ones, are vulnerable to skin cancer. "Cat-safe" sunscreens are available for use on ears and noses to prevent sunburn, but cats tend to lick them off, so they are not highly effective.

NEVER LEAVE YOUR PET IN A WARM CAR.
Heatstroke can develop very quickly in cats who are left in a parked car on a hot day. The temperature rises so rapidly in cars that your cat is at risk of brain damage and death in a very short time.

Giving Medication

Patience is required when giving medication to cats. If they refuse to take it, you can try mixing the medication with a favorite food, or hiding tablets in something the cat finds highly palatable, such as piece of fish or chicken. This will help mask the smell and taste of the medicine. If the cat still refuses the medication, contact your vet for additional suggestions.

6

CARING FOR OLDER CATS

Thanks to significant advances in feline nutrition, medicine, and health care, cats are living longer than ever before. As your cat ages, his behavior and care requirements will also change.

Changes that Come with Aging

Your cat may gradually become less active and his metabolism may slow down as he approaches middle age. You may notice that he sleeps more than he used to. As with humans, cats become more vulnerable to weight gain as they age and may

The older cat deserves special consideration.

need dietary changes to prevent them from becoming obese—with the additional health risks that implies. Your cat will be weighed at visits to the vet's office but you can also weigh him at home to monitor weight gain or loss: weigh yourself on the bathroom scale, do it again holding the cat in your arms, and then subtract to find the cat's weight.

Older cats may benefit from scheduling vet visits every six months or every four months instead of continuing on a schedule of annual check-ups.

An older cat can also become fussy about what she will eat, particularly if she is suffering from dental problems. Moist food may be easier than dry food for her to chew. Since older cats are also prone to kidney problems, the higher water content in moist or canned foods makes it easier to digest. Signs of kidney problems include excessive thirst and weight loss. Your vet may prescribe medication to help improve kidney function.

Older cats are sometimes more comfortable sleeping on a bean bag rather than a standard cat bed. Heated beds are available, but placing an ordinary bed in a warmer part of the house may be sufficient.

If your older cat still likes to go outdoors, make sure you dry him off thoroughly if he returns wet and cold. Older cats may refuse to go out for toileting during the winter so you may need to provide a litter box.

Older cats may experience difficulties with mobility and will appreciate a carefully positioned stool or chair to help them reach their favorite windowsill or lounging spot.

Cats who previously were very adept at grooming themselves may need a little more help in old age, as they become stiffer and less able to turn and reach those awkward places.

Because they are less active, older cats may also need regular claw-clipping, which your vet will be happy to do for you if you are not comfortable doing it yourself. By being vigilant and adaptable, you will ensure that your cat copes well with old age.

Saying Goodbye

Part of the responsibility of caring for your cat means making the difficult decision to have him put to sleep if and when he becomes too ill to enjoy a meaningful quality of life.

Your vet will help and advise you when the time comes to say goodbye, but you can be reassured by the fact that the process will be handled very quickly and sympathetically. Every care is taken to ensure that the cat does not become distressed and, if necessary, a sedative is given first to keep him calm and peaceful. Your vet will then carefully inject the cat with an overdose of anaesthetic.

Many owners choose to bury their cat in their yard. You can ask the vet to dispose of the body if you prefer, or consider using the services of a pet crematorium.

Some owners are comforted by remembering their cat with a permanent reminder such as a plaque or rosebush in his favorite place in the yard.

There is also some evidence that cats from multi-cat households go through their own grieving process at the loss of a companion, so try and offer them reassurance and attention to help compensate for their loss.

Learn More!

www.petwebsite.com

Cat Fanciers' Association
www.cfainc.org

American Veterinary Medical Association
www.avma.org/care4pets

**The American Society for the Prevention
of Cruelty to Animals (ASPCA)**
www.aspca.org

Children will enjoy this **Animaland** site set up by the ASPCA
It includes games, cartoons, fun facts, music, and a section
on cats. Just follow the links: Animal encyclopedia—
Pet Care Guide—Cat.
www.animaland.org